AUSTRALIA

by Darice Bailer

The Child's World

Published by The Child's World®
1980 Lookout Drive • Mankato, MN 56003-1705
800-599-READ • www.childsworld.com

Acknowledgments
The Child's World®: Mary Berendes, Publishing Director
Red Line Editorial: Editorial direction
The Design Lab: Design
Amnet: Production

Design elements: Asaf Eliason/Shutterstock Images;
Shutterstock Images
Photographs ©: Leah-Anne Thompson/Shutterstock Images,
cover (right), 30; Asaf Eliason/Shutterstock Images, cover
(left center), 1 (bottom left), 17 (left); Shutterstock Images,
cover (left top), cover (left bottom), 1 (top), 1 (bottom right),
17 (right), 20, 23; Bill Bachman, 5; iStockphoto, 6–7, 8,
16, 17 (top), 19, 21, 24, 26, 27; Lucy Liu/iStockphoto, 9;
Simon Bradfield/iStockphoto, 11, 14; Chatchai Somwat/
Shutterstock Images, 12; Dan Breckwoldt/Shutterstock
Images, 13; Kokkai Ng/iStockphoto, 25; John Kirk/
iStockphoto, 28; Neale Cousland/Shutterstock Images, 29

ISBN 9781634070379
LCCN 2014959740

Printed in the United States of America
PA02353

ABOUT THE AUTHOR

Darice Bailer has written many books for children. She has visited Australia and has some dear friends who live there. The crocodiles and cassowaries are a little scary, though!

ONE WORLD • MANY COUNTRIES •

TABLE OF CONTENTS

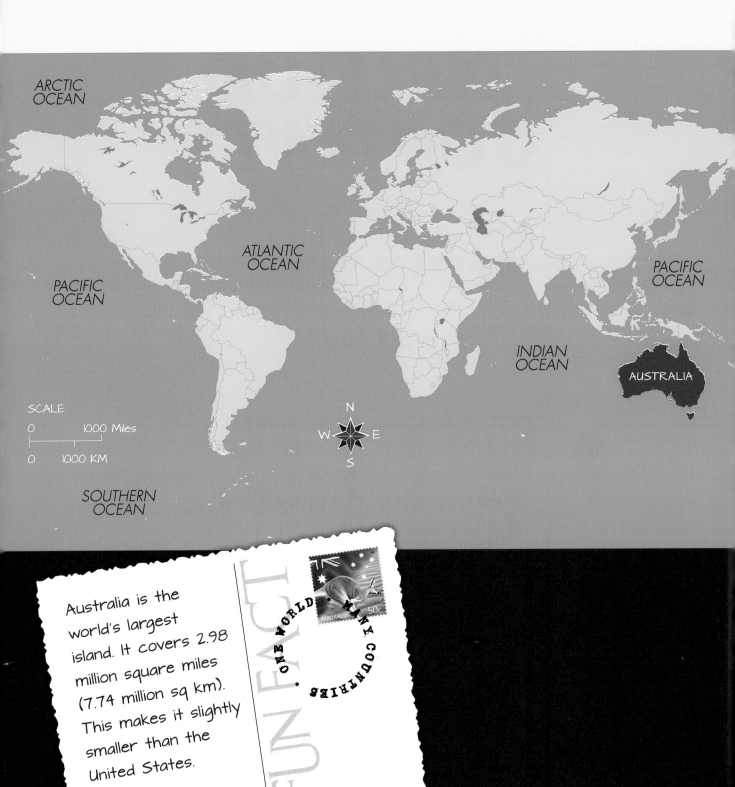

ARCTIC
OCEAN

ATLANTIC
OCEAN

PACIFIC
OCEAN

PACIFIC
OCEAN

INDIAN
OCEAN

AUSTRALIA

SCALE

0   1000 Miles

0   1000 KM

SOUTHERN
OCEAN

N
W   E
S

FUN FACT

ONE WORLD · MANY COUNTRIES

AUSTRALIA   50c

Australia is the
world's largest
island. It covers 2.98
million square miles
(7.74 million sq km).
This makes it slightly
smaller than the
United States.

CHAPTER 1

WELCOME TO AUSTRALIA!

Deep in the desert of the outback, children prepare for school. The nearest schools may be hundreds of miles away. So, many children attend the School of the Air. The school allows students and teachers to connect using computers.

The School of the Air has been teaching students in the outback since 1951. Before computers, students used two-way radios to talk to their teachers.

At 8:30 a.m., children log on to their computers. An icon lets teachers know students are ready for school. The teacher sits in front of a video camera. The children have little cameras on their computers, too.

Students cannot see the other children in their class. They hear their voices, though. Students may finally meet at camp at the end of the year.

The children who attend School of the Air live in Australia. It is the only country that is also a continent. Australia lies below the **equator**. It is in the southern half of the globe. This has

given Australia the nickname the land "Down Under."

Australia belongs to a global family. It is one of 53 countries in the Commonwealth of Nations. The Commonwealth is a group of countries once ruled by the United Kingdom. Now, Australia and the other nations are independent. They have created a country unlike any other.

The Australian outback is a remote area.

CHAPTER 2

THE LAND

As an island, Australia has many beaches. One runs along the Great Ocean Road in Victoria, Australia.

Australia is an island. It is between the South Pacific and Indian oceans. Australia is the smallest of the world's seven continents. It is in the Southern **Hemisphere**.

Australia's location means its seasons are the opposite of those in the United States. When it is winter in Australia, it is summer in the United States. In Australia, winter starts in June. Summer begins in December.

The weather in Australia is hot and dry. It is hottest from December to February. Temperatures can soar above 100 degrees Fahrenheit (38°C). Rainfall is light. Most parts of the island receive less than 20 inches (500 mm) of rain each year.

Australia is the world's flattest continent. Low mountains and plains cover roughly two-thirds of Australia.

An Australian girl admires the Christmas trees she made out of driftwood. In Australia, Christian families often celebrate Christmas by spending the day at the beach.

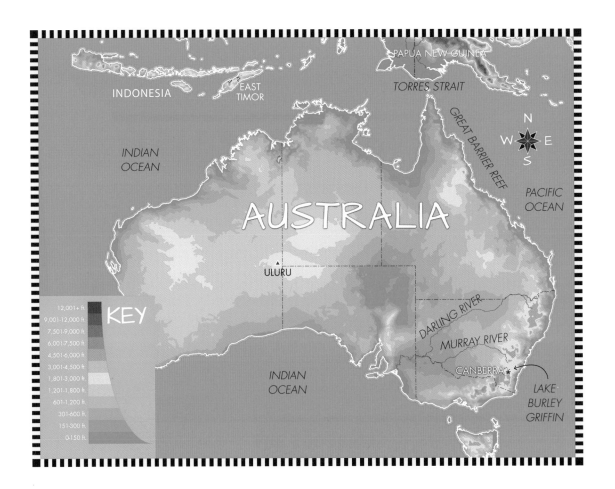

The remaining one-third of the country is a flat, red desert. It is known as the outback.

In the outback there is a famous red rock called Uluru or Ayers Rock. Uluru is as tall as a skyscraper. It is 1.5 miles (2.4 km) wide. Uluru has many caves. Long ago, Australia's native people painted pictures on the rocks inside.

Australia has many precious metals. It is one of the world's richest sources of gold. Opals are also mined there. Gold and

Uluru Rock is made of sandstone. It changes color as the sun moves across the sky. It is most striking in the evening when it is bright orange.

Some of Australia's creatures are dangerous. Twenty of the 25 most venomous snakes on Earth live in Australia. The Sydney funnel-web spider is a venomous hairy spider with fangs. Cassowaries are birds who slash with razor-sharp claws.

opals are two of Australia's biggest **exports**. Australia is also the largest producer of bauxite. It is a rock used to make aluminum.

Australia's land is home to many different animals. There are koalas, kangaroos, and wallabies. The oceans surrounding Australia are filled with creatures, too. The Great Barrier Reef has 1,500 kinds of colorful fish. It is the largest coral reef in the world. Snorkelers and divers see tropical fish, sea turtles, and dugongs at the reef.

CHAPTER 3

GOVERNMENT AND CITIES

Australia's official name is the Commonwealth of Australia. It has six states and two territories. Each state has a capital and government. One of the states is not part of mainland Australia. The state is Tasmania. Tasmania is an island south of Australia.

Australia's lawmakers meet at the Parliament House in Canberra.

Australia's national government is a **constitutional monarchy**. The king or queen of the United Kingdom is head of state. The Australian prime minister is the head of the government.

Australia's capital is Canberra. Australia's leaders discuss national issues and make laws at **Parliament** House, which is located there. Lake Burley Griffin is a beautiful lake at the center of Canberra. It is just north of Parliament House.

The Sydney Opera House is one of Australia's most famous landmarks. The building looks like a boat with sails.

Sydney is Australia's oldest and largest city. It has many famous landmarks. The Sydney Opera House rises along the city's harbor. The Sydney Harbour Bridge is one of the world's longest steel bridges. People can put on safety harnesses and climb to the top of the bridge.

Melbourne is Australia's second-largest city. It is on the Yarra River along Australia's southern coast. About one-quarter of the city contains parks and gardens. The most famous is the Royal Botanic Gardens. It has more than 20,000 kinds of plants.

Australia's land is rich in resources. Miners dig iron ore, coal, copper, and gold out of the ground. Australia is the world's largest exporter of iron ore. Iron ore is used to make iron and steel, creating items from paper clips to skyscraper beams.

Australia also ships coal and natural gas to other countries where it is used for energy. No country exports more coal than Australia. Four out of Australia's five biggest trading partners are in Asia. They are China, Japan, the Republic of Korea, and Singapore.

A large conveyor moves coal in New South Wales, Australia.

The Royal Flying Doctor Service has a fleet of airplanes ready for emergencies in the outback. The insides of the planes have been transformed into flying operating rooms or intensive care units. Pilots, doctors, and nurses take off and pick up Australians who are hurt or sick in remote areas.

FUN FACT

ONE WORLD • MANY COUNTRIES

Australia's currency

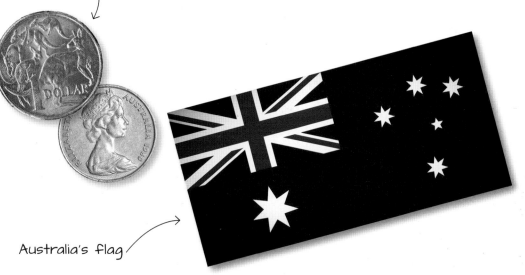

Australia's flag

GLOBAL CONNECTIONS

Inventions people use every day, such as Google Maps, come from Australia. Google Maps has mapped trillions of streets all over the planet. Google Maps software was created at Google Australia in Sydney.

Another invention people use every day is Wi-Fi. Australian researchers helped develop high-speed wireless Internet. They found a better way to send data signals. This allows people to surf the Internet from smart phones, tablets, and laptops without a cord.

Another Australian invention flies around the world every day on airplanes. It is called the cockpit voice recorder, or black box. An Australian scientist invented it. The box records pilots' voices and other sounds on the plane.

If a plane crashes, investigators hunt for the black box. It is not black, though. The box is bright orange to help investigators find it. The box is strong. It can even survive a fire. Listening to the voices and sounds helps explain what went wrong.

CHAPTER 4

PEOPLE AND CULTURES

A woman dressed in traditional Aboriginal face paint and clothing

Aborigines were the first people to live in Australia. By the late 1700s, between 250,000 and 500,000 Aborigines lived on the island. Australia's other early settlers arrived from the Torres Strait Islands. These islands are north of Queensland, Australia.

In 1770, an English captain named James Cook sailed along the east coast of Australia. He claimed the land for England. England began to send its **convicts** to Australia.

The convicts in Australia did not live in jails. They built homes and planted fruits and vegetables. A small number of the early settlers were free people who were excited to live in this new land. During the 1830s, England encouraged more people to move to Australia. They were needed to work on farms and ranches.

Australia's population has roots from countries all over the globe.

Australia's next big wave of settlers arrived after World War II (1939–1945). After the war, Europe's cities were badly damaged and homes were destroyed. Australia needed workers. Europeans and people from all over the world came to Australia.

These settlers often took Aboriginal lands. In 1967, Aborigines finally became citizens of Australia. They now had the right to vote. In 2008, the government apologized to the Aborigines for mistreating them.

Aboriginal hunters often used boomerangs. They are flat pieces of wood shaped like a wide letter "v." Hunters threw them at wild game. Today, boomerangs are used in competitions that measure speed and accuracy.

FUN FACT

ONE WORLD • MANY COUNTRIES

Today, Australians come from about 200 countries. Most of Australia's **immigrants** come from New Zealand. Many others arrive from India, China, the Philippines, Vietnam, Malaysia, Sri Lanka, and Iraq. People come for the country's good schools, jobs, freedom, and opportunities.

Australia's laws guarantee religious freedom for everyone. More than half of all Australians are Christian. Australians are also Buddhist, Muslim, Hindu, and Jewish.

English is the national language. Australia's Aborigines speak native languages depending on where they live. Some Aboriginal children might not learn English until they start school.

Aboriginals believe that the spirits of their **ancestors** came to Earth and created rivers and mountains. They call this time of creation the Dreamtime. Aboriginals tell stories about how the sun was created or how birds got their colors. These legends are part of their religion.

On January 26, people celebrate Australia Day. It is a national holiday. Australia Day marks the day in 1788 when the

The *didgeridoo* is a traditional instrument used by Aborigines during spiritual ceremonies.

Australian children wave flags as they march in an Anzac Day parade in Mackay.

first British settlers arrived in Sydney. The country celebrates with picnics and fireworks.

Anzac Day is another national holiday. "Anzac" stands for the Australian and New Zealand Army Corps. On April 25, Australians remember the brave soldiers who fought in wars. On Anzac Day, soldiers march in a parade. People in the crowd wave flags and say thank you.

CHAPTER 5

DAILY LIFE

Australia is a sunny country with nearly 11,000 beaches. Most Australians live within a half-hour drive from the beach. From mid-December until late January, children have a school break. Families often to go to the beach during that time.

Girls take a surfing lesson at Wollongong North Beach.

These Australian lifeguards patrol the beach in a four-wheeler. Each year, the country's lifeguards help more than 1 million people.

Lifeguards dressed in red and yellow watch swimmers. The ocean's strong currents can pull swimmers out to sea. Surf Life Saving clubs in Australia teach water safety and help swimmers in trouble.

Most Australians live in houses or apartments in towns. Everyday clothing in Australia is similar to that worn in the United States. People often wear T-shirts and blue jeans. At school, many children wear uniforms.

Modern homes in Australia

There is a great variety of food in Australia. Along the coasts, seafood is common. Many Australians also enjoy grilling steaks, hamburgers, and sausages on barbecues. Pies filled with meats, vegetables, and gravy are also popular.

Australians have many ways to travel. Cars are the most common form of transportation. Large cities have light rail trains, trams, subways, and buses. Ferries carry people across Sydney Harbour.

To travel across the country, people can fly or take trains. The Indian Pacific is a train running between Perth and Sydney. The cross-country trip takes a little longer than two days. The Ghan Railroad runs through the middle of Australia. It is a two-day trip from Darwin in the north to Adelaide in the south.

Millions of visitors travel to Australia every year. They often like to see the famous Sydney Opera House or the colorful fish at the Great Barrier Reef. From dangerous crocodiles to adorable koalas, Australia is filled with wildlife and adventure.

A train leaves the station at Alice Springs and travels on the Ghan Railroad.

DAILY LIFE FOR CHILDREN

Children begin a new school year in late January. Many students wear uniforms to school. Students also wear floppy hats outdoors. The sun's rays are very strong and harmful near the equator. In schools there's a "no hat, no play" rule.

Because of the warm weather, Australian kids love being outdoors. Boys and girls play cricket in schoolyards. Cricket is sport that is a little like baseball. The bat is wide and flat, like a paddle. The pitcher is called a bowler.

Vegemite is a popular food in Australia. It is a spread made of yeast, vegetables, and spices. People eat it on bread, toast, or crackers.

FUN FACT · ONE WORLD · MANY COUNTRIES ·

FAST FACTS

Population: 23 million

Area: 2.96 million square miles (7.74 million sq km)

Capital: Canberra

Largest Cities: Sydney, Melbourne, and Brisbane

Form of Government: Constitutional Monarchy

Language: English

Trading Partners: China, Japan, and South Korea

Major Holidays: Australia Day and Anzac Day

National Dish: Vegemite (a paste made of brewers' yeast, vegetables, and spices that is spread on bread, toast, and crackers)

A boy celebrates Australia Day near Sydney Harbour.

GLOSSARY

ancestors (AN-sess-ters) Ancestors are people in a family who lived a long time ago. Ancestors are an important part of spiritual life for Aborigines.

constitutional monarchy (kon-stuh-TOO-shun-uhl MON-ar-key) A constitutional monarchy is a government with a king or queen who acts as the head of state and a parliament to make and pass laws. Australia is a constitutional monarchy.

convicts (KON-victs) Convicts are people who have been proven guilty of crimes. The United Kingdom shipped convicts to Australia.

equator (i-KWAY-tor) The equator is an imaginary line around the middle of the earth, halfway between the North Pole and South Pole. Australia is on the equator.

exports (EX-ports) An export is food, clothing, or other goods that one country sells to other countries. Australia exports beef and veal.

hemisphere (HEM-uss-fihr) A hemisphere is half a sphere, or half of Earth. The whole continent of Australia is in the Southern Hemisphere.

immigrants (IM-uh-grunts) Immigrants are people who move to live permanently in a country. Many immigrants come to Australia from New Zealand and Asia.

parliament (PAR-luh-ment) Parliament is a group that makes laws. Australians vote for members of parliament.

To Learn More

BOOKS

Scillian, Devin. *D is for Down Under: An Australia Alphabet*. Ann Arbor, MI: Sleeping Bear Press, 2010.

Scott, Janine, and Peter Rees. *Australia: Everything You Ever Wanted to Know*. Victoria, Australia: Lonely Planet Publications, 2012.

WEB SITES

Visit our Web site for links about Australia: **childsworld.com/links**

Note to Parents, Teachers, and Librarians: We routinely verify our Web links to make sure they are safe and active sites. So encourage your readers to check them out!

Index